HOW TO DRAW CUTE BEARS

LEARNING STEP BY STEP HOW TO CREATE BEAUTIFUL ANIMALS CHIBI VERSION FROM A CIRCLE

MERÚ ILLUSTRATIONS

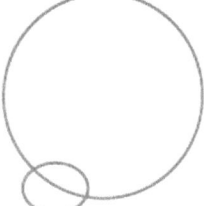

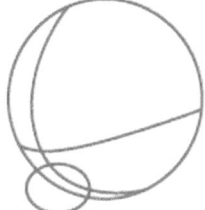

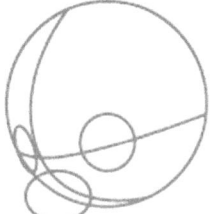

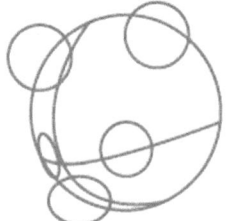

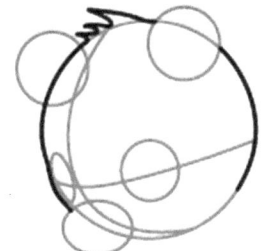

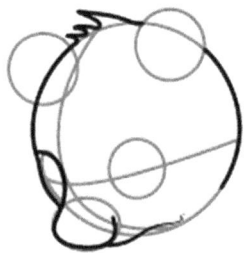

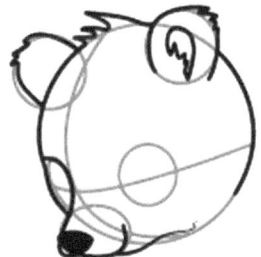

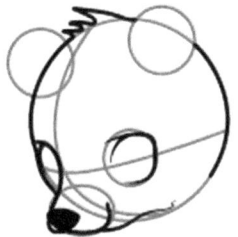

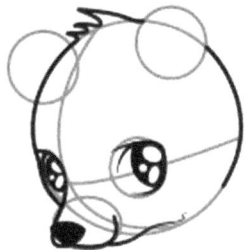

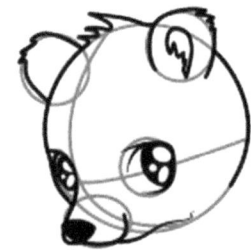

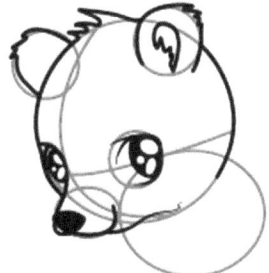

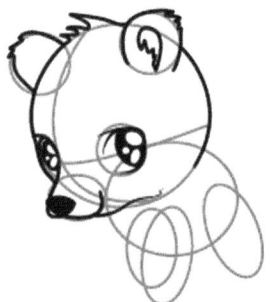

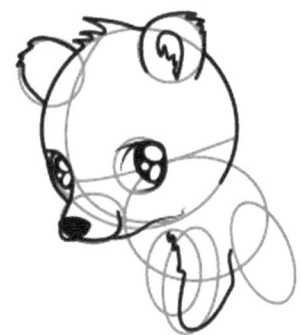

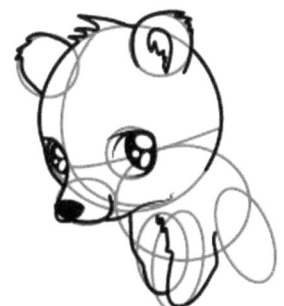

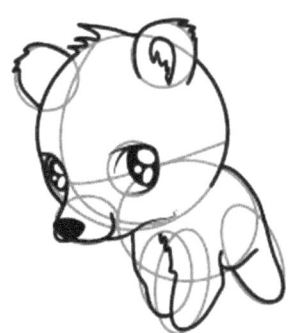

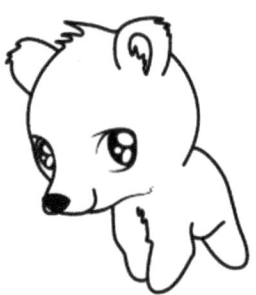

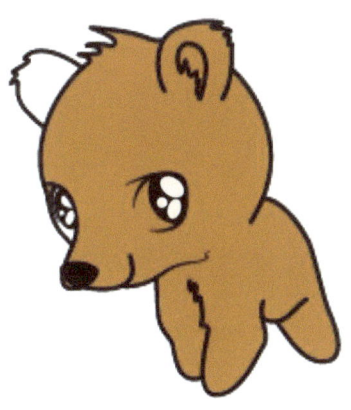

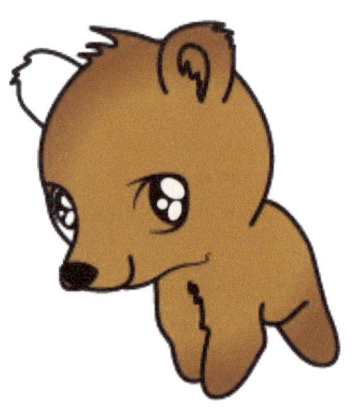

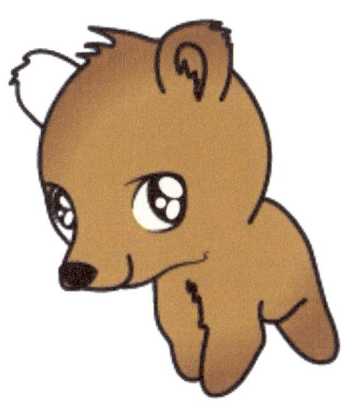

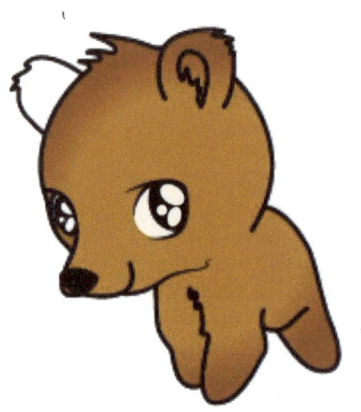

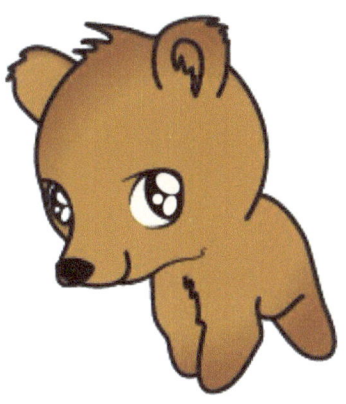

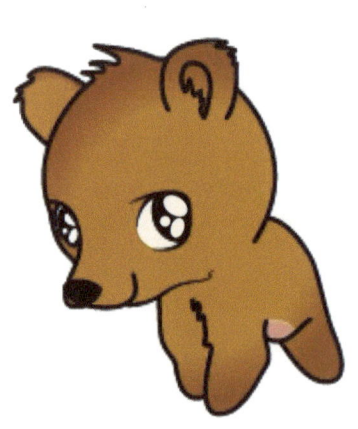

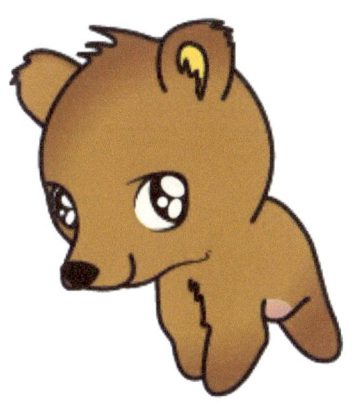

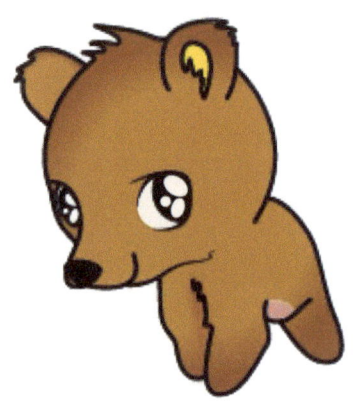

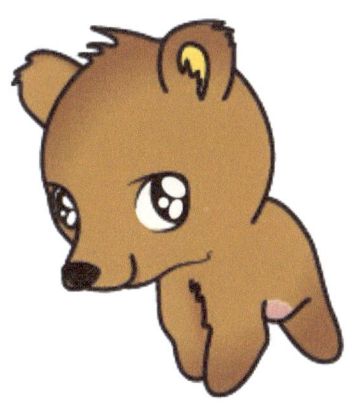

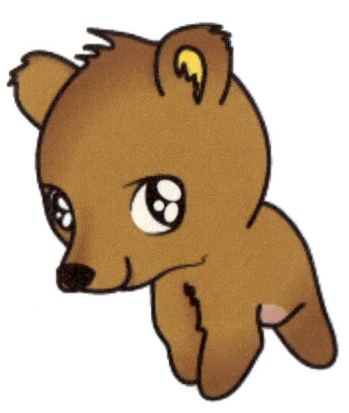

www.ingramcontent.com/pod-product-compliance
Lightning Source LLC
Chambersburg PA
CBHW041211180526
45172CB00006B/1234